Women's Financial Wisdom

How to Become a Woman of Wealth

Ivy Gilbert-Vigue

Published by Fifth Avenue Publishing
730 Fifth Avenue, 9th Floor
New York, NY 10019
1-800-992-6616

Printed in the United States
123456789

ISBN 0-9629858-1-3

TABLE OF CONTENTS

ACKNOWLEDGMENTS

"No one can be the best at everything,
but when all of us combine our talents,
we can be the best at virtually anything."
Don Ward

I want to thank my parents, Graydon and Jane Gilbert, for their endless love, support and belief in me. Through this, they have taught me to believe in myself and my abilities. My father always told me to be a leader and not a follower, and this one statement has influenced everything I have done.

When I read the above quote by Don Ward, I think about combining my love with the love of three very special individuals -- my children, Kristopher and Kailyn, and my husband, Jim. They all bring happiness and love to my life daily. My children are full of hopes, dreams and aspirations. These dreams are never hindered by doubt or negativity, and their enthusiasm for life is unmatched. Through them I see the beauty of life that we are born to see.

Without my husband, Jim Vigue, I would not be pursuing my dreams. Jim has given me the strength and encouragement to become all that I am capable of becoming. His relentless support of personal growth is unmatched, and he has loved me through each stage of my own growth. He is my mentor, my best friend, and the love of my life.

Women's Financial Wisdom

How to Become a Woman of Wealth

PART I

INTRODUCTION

"Unless you try to do something beyond
what you have already mastered,
you will never grow."
Ronald E. Osborn

I believe we all have a purpose in life, and from an early age I knew mine had something to do with finances. I was never an Alex P. Keaton, mind you, but I always did have a head for numbers.

I also was a motivated worker. Even as a teen you could find me baby-sitting, scooping ice-cream at the beach in the summer, or working at a local craft shop after school. I liked the idea of having my own money and savings. By the time I graduated from high school I had saved several thousand dollars, unlike most of my friends, who had to scrimp to find $10 to go to the movies. I knew I had a knack for budgeting, saving and planning, but I was not sure what I would do with this talent.

As the years went on, my path lead me to a financial planning firm where I not only fell in love with my future husband, but where I also fell in love with the financial industry.

I spent ten years managing the company's finances, running the brokerage operation, and working with male financial advisors in handling their largest clients. I was very good at what I did, yet something troubled me. In 1990, I finally realized what it was.

I was troubled by the fact that fewer women than men enlisted the help of financial advisors. Those who did seemed intimidated and frustrated by the experience. Time after time I would watch these women walk away from a consultation not fully understanding what they were doing and why. They left with a sense of lack of control. It wasn't that the male advisors they had consulted were poor ones; in fact, they were very good. It was something much deeper. These women walked away feeling powerless as to their financial situation.

I don't think these women fully understood why they felt so frustrated and powerless. They would look at it rationally and decide to take more control by learning more about what they were doing -- but this often wasn't enough. The feelings went much deeper than that, and they could not quite put it all together.

As a result, I decided to focus my energy and time helping women. I started a newsletter called *Women & Investing*, combining aspects of a woman's home, business and financial life. I gave seminars and taught courses to try to educate more women to the fact that they needed to begin taking control over their financial affairs, and I developed my own financial planning practice, specializing in assisting women. But I still didn't feel it was enough.

A few years later, Deane Whitney, a financial advisor with whom I had worked with for 14 years, came to me. I had learned much from Deane over the years and respected him immensely. He told me that it was time I figured out what the real need was, and then fill it. This statement stayed with me, and I now feel it is time for me to fill that need. I wrote this book to give women a place to start, and to teach them the steps they need to take in order to gain financial control and independence.

I hope this book will help many women gain insight into where they have been, where they are now, and how to start moving forward.

~1~

MEMORIES

Our past provides lessons.
Learn from them.

"The greatest thing in this world
is not so much where we are,
but in what direction
we are moving."
Oliver Wendell Holmes

I remember growing up to stories of my great-great grandmother and her dowry. Her parents placed valuables in a wooden chest that her father had made for her. Her mother placed into the box fine china, a set of silver candlesticks and the finest linens she had ever seen. She was very proud of this chest. She knew that the ability to provide her new husband with such valuables brought pride to her family. On the day she was married the chest was presented to her new husband. He loaded it on his wagon among his possessions, and they began their journey to their new home and life.

I remembered thinking, "Why did it become *his* possession and not grandmother's? And why didn't *he* give grandmother a special box?" I was later told that in those days a woman had no rights of ownership.

Years later I received a hope chest of my own. The box was finely crafted, and the smell of cedar permeated my room when I opened it. I thought of how this box may have been similar to my great-great grandmother's -- a simple wooden box, symbolizing a family's tradition of dowries, marriage, and financial ownership from prior years.

We think we have come so far since those days. But how far have we truly come?

Think back to *your* grandmother's day. In most households the male handled all of the finances. He paid the bills, took care of all banking and made all of the investments. Women had rights of ownership but weren't considered competent enough to handle financial matters. Often the only money our grandmothers were allowed to control was the grocery money. With this, however, they proved to be very competent. They would often be able to buy groceries, scrimp and save a little here and there, and tuck some away for emergencies.

This bit of savings was all some women ever had of their own. They would then tuck away whatever they could save in a secret hiding place. Many times this hiding place was in a small purse under their mattress. This is where the term *mattress stuffer* came from. Some chose a canister in the back of the cupboard or a shoe box pushed to the back of a closet shelf. I have even heard that some women would bury their savings in their back yards.

This small token of cash ownership was all these women had to call their own. To them it was their *security blanket*, and it needed to be safe.

Women still hide money to this day -- maybe not to the extreme of burying it, but in places they consider to be *safe* for emergencies.

Besides having a safe place for these funds, there was a need to hide their savings effort. They were afraid to let anyone know that they had saved any money for fear it would have to be given up. It was almost as if women back then understood the need for accepting financial responsibility for themselves and seemed to be grasping at whatever small amount of control they could obtain.

Today the poverty rate for older women has risen dramatically -- 65% live below the poverty level.* This is what has happened to a generation of women who took no control over their financial affairs.

---

*National Center for Women & Retirement Research (NCWRR)

STEP 1:

Begin changing the past by remembering what has taken place. Make a commitment to yourself not to relive the past, but to move forward in a positive, responsible manner.

~2~

EMOTIONAL BARRICADES

Have we been left with no control? Our only limits are those that are self-imposed.

"No one can make you feel inferior
without your consent."
Eleanor Roosevelt

How do you think women felt when they were not thought competent enough to handle financial matters?

When I asked dozens of women from earlier generations this question, the most frequently given answer was they didn't feel capable of handling such items and were thankful not to have the responsibility.

Years of conditioning had taught them they weren't capable of handling financial matters. They were conditioned from birth, and from all prior generations, that their role in life was to be a nurturer, and the husband would take care of the financial issues. They believed that this was a much too complicated area, and they *shouldn't fill their pretty heads* with such worries. *Women were not good at math*, and they should let their husband take care of them and their financial well being. This began their belief of financial incompetence.

This sense of incompetence and dependence lead to great fear of taking responsibility for their financial affairs. Women were fearful that they *couldn't* handle the financial role and were happy not to have the burden of such a chore. They looked upon household finances as something that was much too difficult for them to comprehend.

Now, I am certain that these women were very bright and easily could have learned how to pay bills and manage the household funds; however, it was not something that women were taught or encouraged to do. It was considered downright unladylike.

Today, most of us pay our own bills, have a savings and checking account, and often have a few investments. Statistics tell us, however, that far too many women are overly cautious and conservative in their investment strategy. We remain fearful of financial risk and of losing our money.

Women have been without control for so long that we feel we must prove we are competent to handle money. This is why we tend to be overly conservative and cautious. In a manner of speaking, we are still mattress stuffers -- maybe not literally, yet we are trying to prove that we know how to keep our money as safe as our male counterparts did years ago, which causes us to go overboard in our cautiousness.

Fear is a powerful force. Originally women were fearful of handling money. Now women are fearful that they will not handle it properly, or they will be perceived to have mishandled it. The fear has simply evolved and adapted to a new era.

Because fear is such an uncomfortable state, we often simply ignore it. This has caused even more anxiety over money. Proving checkbooks, handling credit card debt, and taking responsibility for our own financial future takes a back seat until a crisis forces us to address these issues.

To avoid this feeling of fear, we indulge in *magical thinking*, believing that everything will take care of itself. This will not happen. Magical thinking will not pay for those items that we just put on our credit card, and will not prove our checkbook for us. We need to take control of our spending and cash flow. By doing this we can begin to overcome this feeling of fear, and we will start moving toward confident management of our money.

Fear is simply an illusion and a sign that we need to pay more attention. Once we remove this illusion of fear, it will be easier to proceed.

STEP 2:

Remove all illusions your fears have created. You can overcome any fear you may have. By facing your fears and your financial weaknesses, you will be able to put them into perspective and begin to move forward.

~3~

A WOMAN'S WORTH

Whatever women feel they are worth is probably a lot less than their true worth.

"It is essential to understand
that there is a vast difference between
being inadequate and feeling inadequate."
Yvonne Kaye

When I think about a woman's worth I think back to the old *I Love Lucy* shows. Lucy's neighbor Ethel never had anything new. All she ever wanted was a new dress, but her husband, Fred, who handled all of the financial matters, didn't feel she needed one; therefore, she never got one. Throughout the years the show ran, Fred always determined whether Ethel received any funds for items she needed. To me, Fred was dictating Ethel's worth and value. Ethel rationalized it by thinking Fred was a tightwad.

Even though Ethel appeared not to let it bother her when Fred would withhold funds, what do you think it did to her sense of self-worth? What about her self-esteem?

Ethel was not the only woman whose financial worth was dictated by her spouse. This was typical in many households during that era. If I asked you what you feel you are worth on an annual basis for the work you do, what dollar figure would you give me? $25,000? $50,000? $100,000? Most of us respond with whatever we are making in the work force. If we do not work outside the home, the dollar amount drops dramatically.

For many years a *woman's place was considered to be in the home*. It was rare that a woman earned money of her own simply because she didn't work outside of the home. Her role was that of a nurturer. It was her responsibility to take care of the home and family. Unfortunately, no financial value was placed on this work. As a result, these women did not feel that they had *earned* any money, nor *earned* the right to make decisions as to how the household money was to be handled.

We are now earning pay outside of the home, yet we still have a hard time giving ourselves credit and placing value on what we do inside of the home. Until we begin to understand our own worth, we will never be able to accept the idea of having wealth in our lives.

Most women were raised as *givers*, not *receivers.* We were taught that if we believed we *deserved* financial rewards or compensation for our work, we would be considered greedy or selfish. This misconception stands between women and wealth.

Many of my friends and clients have absolutely everything going for them: intelligence, talent, looks, ambition and much more. The only problem is they always have a financial crisis. If they feel they have more than the next guy, they feel greedy and self-destruct. If they ask for a raise, they feel selfish and sabotage the raise. They have not yet been able to place a value on themselves. They do not have a sense of their own worth. As a result, their beliefs control their behaviors, and ultimately, create the distance between them and financial security.

As a financial advisor I always ask numerous questions of my clients. One question I ask is related to life insurance. Many women tell me they are married and do not need any insurance coverage. I then ask the following questions:

- Do you work?
- How much do you make annually?
- How much of this covers household expenses?
- How much goes toward savings?
- Do you have any debt?
- Do you have children?
- Would your spouse have to hire daycare for your children should something happen to you?
- Do you take care of the home?

- Would you have to hire cleaners or others to take care of the home if you didn't do it?

The list goes on and on.

I then ask them to calculate the following:

Add together:

Gross Wages earned outside the home	$_____
Any additional costs to your family should you die, such as additional day care or household costs to cover what you do now for no pay.	$_____
Total	$_____
Divide this result by .08	.08

(Note: I use .08 because I assume you could obtain an 8% interest rate on your money. If you could only obtain 6%, divide by .06).

Equals	$_____

The answer gives you an idea of what you would need to replace your worth annually.

Let me give you an example:

Ann makes $42,000 a year as a nurse. If she died, her family would need an additional $3,000 a year to cover added daycare. Add these two together to get the value of Ann's financial contribution to the household. Divide the $45,000 by .08 and you will get $562,500. This is what Ann is financially worth to her family. $562,500 times 8% per year is $45,000, or what she was contributing to her household annually.

If you don't work outside of the home, place a value on the work you do at home. You'll need to come up with a job description like the one stated below and place an estimated value by each area that applies. Then simply add the values together.

Job Description

Child Care Provider	$______
Housekeeper	$______
Full Time Cook	$______
Taxi Driver	$______
Laundress	$______
Seamstress	$______
Shopper	$______
Pet Caretaker	$______
Other	$______

This simple calculation helps women begin to recognize exactly what it would take to replace their financial contribution to their households.

Determine your own financial self worth, and tell yourself daily that you are worth it. Write it down and put it where you will see it often. Begin to internalize that you are worth the value you have placed on yourself.

The more you believe this, the more you will be able to take actions that will guide you to the financial security you deserve. Your beliefs control your actions, and your actions control your future.

STEP 3

Calculate an estimated value of your financial worth. Once you have a dollar amount, accept that you are worth this, plus much more. You need to believe that you are *a woman of worth.*

~4~

BREAKING THE MOLD

Breaking the mold of your past will be the beginning of building your new, true self.

"Think and feel yourself there!
To achieve any aim in life, you need
to project the end result....
Think of the elation, the satisfaction, the joy!
Carrying the ecstatic feeling will bring
the desired goal into view."
Grace Speare

Imagine having a plaster cast made of your body. Every inch of you is covered with plaster-of-Paris. It dries slowly, but as it dries, your body begins to feel tight, restricted and unable to move. Even though you may want to change your position or take a step, you are unable to do so.

This feeling is similar to years of conditioning. Slowly, layer by layer and thought by thought, your past conditioning, actions and beliefs have built the mold you are wearing today. Once you recognize that you have built this mold for yourself, however, it is much easier to break it down.

First, you must *want* to break this mold, and second, you must truly believe you are *worth* the time and effort. These two items will give you the strength you need to begin chipping away at your constricting plaster cast.

By breaking free of old thought patterns you can begin to *crack your plaster*. You may start with tiny movements, but as the plaster begins to crack, it falls away, and soon you realize that you can once again move freely. You no longer feel restricted or unable to change or move. This will encourage you to take another step forward.

We need to put the past behind us just like an old cast, not only for ourselves, but for our daughters and granddaughters. Future generations of women need to know that they are *women of worth.*

Let me share a few statistics with you:

- 50% of women will divorce. [1]
- 60% of single mothers live in poverty. [2]
- The average age of widowhood in the United States is 56. [3]
- Nearly 65% of elderly women live below the poverty level. [4]
- 80-90% of women find themselves financially on their own at some point in their lives. [5]
- 80% of women are left in financial jeopardy due to divorce or widowhood. [6]

---

1. The National Center for Women and Retirement Research (NCWRR)
2. Margaret Chase Smith Center for Public Policy Survey
3. The National Center for Women and Retirement Research (NCWRR)
4. The National Center for Women and Retirement Research (NCWRR)
5. Oppenheimer Funds Survey, March 1992
6. The National Center for Women and Retirement Research (NCWRR)

Now, allow me to tell you two stories:

Alice, age 52, and Paul, age 53, had three children ages 13, 15, and 18. Paul earned $85,000 per year, and Alice didn't work outside of the home. They had purchased a new house two years ago and still had a $180,000 mortgage on it. Their total expenses equaled 90% of Paul's income. Their only savings were in Paul's retirement plan at work, which had approximately $130,000 in it. Paul had a life insurance policy for $250,000. Paul died unexpectedly in a car accident.

Alice was faced with the following:

- Alice was only 52, not 59 1/2, the IRS retirement age. If she were to use the funds in Paul's retirement plan, she may have been subject to a 10% penalty, and she would be using her only resource for retirement income.

- She was given $250,000 as a life insurance death benefit. She could use the $250,000 to cover her annual expenses; however, if she maintained her current lifestyle, these funds would most likely run out after 5 years. She also wanted to provide her children with the financial resources to attend college. This would deplete these funds even sooner.

- She considered investing the $250,000 so that she could receive a steady income without using the principal, yet $250,000 invested at 8% generated only $20,000 per year versus the $76,500 ($85,000 x 90%) that she needed.

Alice was faced with a financial crisis. She could no longer meet her financial obligations, she was forced to sell her house, and she was forced to change her family's lifestyle dramatically.

This scenario is extremely common. The amounts may vary, but the results are the same -- too many women are left in financial jeopardy due to widowhood.

Then there is Sylvia. Sylvia is 76 years old. She had saved for retirement, yet as the years went by, her savings were depleted. Sylvia now lives on Social Security in the amount of $8,500 per year. She can pay for her basic needs, yet when her refrigerator breaks down, her dentures need repair, or the holidays come, she finds herself in a state of depression and desperation. Every time I see her, she begs me to tell everyone I know about her, so that others do not find themselves in a similar situation when they are older.

Sylvia is not alone in her financial situation. Approximately two out of three elderly women in the United States live just like she does.

This is what has happened to a generation of women who took no control over their financial future. If nothing I've said before gives you the motivation to begin taking control of your financial affairs and putting your old ways of thinking and acting behind you, I hope these statistics will give you the incentive you need. As you can see, the old way of thinking has just not worked for women. If it had, there would not be two out of every three women in financial jeopardy after divorce or widowhood. Had women taken some control over their financial affairs, these statistics would not be so high, and women would not be paying the consequences for inadequate planning.

It is time to change the course of history, and we need to begin one step at a time, and one woman at a time. Why not let it begin with you? It is time for you to begin taking responsibility for your financial situation, whatever it may be. You are not going to place blame, or dwell on the past. You will remember and understand your past, and let it go. Then you will be ready to face the present and take your first step forward.

STEP 4

Continue to chip away at the financial mold that has encased your thoughts and beliefs about money until it begins to crack. Then you can break free of the beliefs that no longer serve you. It is time to replace these old beliefs with new facts so you can move forward into the future in a positive and productive manner.

~5

THE KEY TO KNOWLEDGE

We have the knowledge necessary, but it is worthless unless put into practice.

*"There are precious few
Einsteins among us.
Most brilliance arises from
ordinary people working together in
extraordinary ways."*
Grace Speare

There are two secrets to financial knowledge. The first is that you need very little of it. All you need to know is how to ask the right questions. The second secret is simply to be open to learning and willing to start at the beginning.

You don't have to be a scholar in the financial field or an Albert Einstein, but you must be someone who has broken free of the past and is now willing to seek the steps to take. You will *not* have to become a *Wall Street expert*. I promise!

Today, the financial industry is so complex that there really are no true experts in the field. In order to be considered an expert, one must concentrate only in one small area of financial planning. Most good financial advisors will tell you that they work with a team of specialists and experts. One may specialize in insurance, one in the stock market, another in college or retirement planning, and yet another in estate planning.

It is virtually impossible to know it all. Even the experts do not know all there is to know. This should help remove some of the intimidation that financial planning holds for you.

The trick is to simply become a generalist. Know a little about a lot. This is the key to beginning. To do this, you can read books on a particular subject, attend seminars, take adult education courses, or speak with a financial advisor who will help educate you.

If you have determined to put the past behind you and move forward, you have a lot of choices at this point in your life. You know that you are capable of handling your financial affairs, plus you realize that you are *worth* the time and effort. You can choose whether you want to learn about the necessary topics in depth, or you can choose a good financial partner to help with the details.

Many of you will *choose* to utilize a financial advisor to help handle your finances. You don't have to do everything yourself to be financially independent.

That is not what this term means. Having a financial partner and making *joint* decisions may be the means that is best for you to become financially independent. All you want to do is take part in the process and take control of the end results.

Having knowledge doesn't necessarily mean you have to know everything yourself. Webster's Dictionary describes knowledge as, "The result or condition of knowing; clear perception, learning, information."

Break this down for a moment.....

"The result or condition of knowing" -- You know that you need to begin to take some control over your financial situation.

"Clear perception" -- perception is just an idea or understanding of an idea created in your mind. Know exactly what result you want to obtain.

"Learning" --- We all learn something new daily. You now need to learn something about your finances daily. As long as you are acquiring a bit of knowledge, no matter how insignificant it may seem, you are learning and moving forward.

"Information" -- Information can be learned. This area of the definition of knowledge may simply imply that you have learned where to find information when you need it.

When you break down the definition of knowledge according to Webster's Dictionary, it shows us that knowledge really is quite easy to obtain. In fact, many of us have a lot of it already. You probably have a lot more than you give yourself credit.

So where do you go from here? Are you feeling a bit more confident about moving forward, yet still don't feel comfortable in doing it all yourself? It is now time to begin learning.

STEP 5

Make a commitment to obtain one small bit of knowledge each day. Do not be intimidated by knowledge or by those who appear to have more of it than you. Learn from these people, and soon you will be one of them.

~6~

THE ART OF ASKING

Questioning does not show a lack of trust. It shows that we trust ourselves enough to seek the answers we need.

*"You may be disappointed if you fail,
but you are doomed if you
don't try."*
Beverly Sills

As young children we begin questioning everything around us with the infamous, "*What's that?*" Once this question is satisfied, we start with *"Why?"*

As a parent I remember those record breaking questioning sessions. My two-year-old would sit at the dinner table and look at her peas and say, *"What's that?"* I would respond with, *"Those are peas. Now eat them up."* This was definitely the wrong thing to say to a two-year-old because it was an open invitation for the *Why Questioning Session.* Our conversation would sound something like this:

"Eat your peas."
"Why?"
"Because they are good for you."
"Why?"
"Because they help you to grow up big and strong."
"Why?"
"Because they have vitamins in them."

"Why?"
"Because they are a vegetable."
"Why?"
"Because God made them that way."
"Why?"
"Because He did!"
"Why?"
"AGHHHH - Just eat your peas!"

Maybe you remember some of those sessions. Two-year-olds have the art of asking questions down to a science. They are better at it than any talk show host could ever imagine. If police ever wanted to crack a criminal into confessing his crime, all they would have to do is put him in a room with a two year old to ask the questions for a few hours.

Somehow along the way, however, we stopped asking questions. The *whys* stopped being asked, and the *who, what, when* and *where* disappeared from our vocabulary.

Some believe it happens when we go to school. A fear overtakes us as we begin to raise our hand in class to ask a question. Our throat begins to dry and our heart pounds hard. As our hand begins to raise above our head we decide we don't want to risk asking a dumb question and quickly lower it, but it is too late. The teacher has already seen it and stops and calls on us. The room quiets and all eyes are on us as we ask the question. We hear snickers and giggling and want to crawl under the desk to avoid feeling so *stupid*.

As a result of this humiliating experience, we stop asking questions. This experience stifles our questioning ability forever. As we mature and enter relationships, we call our lack of questioning..... *TRUST*.

I have counseled numerous women of all ages, many recently divorced or widowed, some contemplating divorce, and many married and simply looking to begin taking control over their financial future. I ask each of them many questions, and I am always surprised to hear an answer I get all too often.

I ask questions such as, *How much money does your spouse make? How is your money currently invested, how much does your spouse have in his retirement plan, how big is your mortgage, how much insurance coverage does your spouse have?* When I get the answer, *"I don't know."* I then put on my *two-year-old* hat and ask, *"Why?"*

This is when I get that heart wrenching answer, *"I never asked."* I must always look like I am in shock

because each of them tries to explain by stating, *"I **trusted** or **trust** him with these matters."*
I am not advocating a lack of trust. I am advocating *asking.* As I have previously stated, knowledge is power, and having knowledge gives you the edge you need in order to go forward. The easiest way to obtain knowledge is by asking questions.

You may have a difficult time asking your spouse or partner about specific financial information. You might find that he reacts with anger and makes the assumption that you do not trust him. If this happens, reassure him that you fully trust him, but want to help out in this area and cannot do so unless you learn. Let him know that you want to use his expertise in your learning effort.

You might also find that your partner is thrilled that you want to learn and take on some of the responsibility. If this is the case, work together and review everything, and then decide who should handle each area.

In either case, start slowly. Write a list of questions and address them one at a time. Don't attack or make accusations. Try to work together. If you find your spouse or partner is not cooperative at all, it will be up to you to begin your research. Monitor the mail for statements, speak to your insurance agent regarding your coverage, and if you know who your investment manager is, give him or her a call and arrange to review your portfolio.

Again, keep in mind these statistics:

- 50% of women will divorce.
- The average age of widowhood in the U.S. is 56.
- 80-90% of women find themselves financially on their own financially at some point in their lives.

We may not *want* to manage and control our assets, yet we may *have* to do so. With statistics like those listed above, it is almost guaranteed that we will have to manage our own financial affairs. The *question*s you must ask yourself are:

Do I want to learn now, or do I want to learn as a result of a crisis?

Do I want to be forced to learn while I am dealing emotionally with a divorce or widowhood?

If you were to ask me these questions, I would tell you that I would rather learn now.

It really isn't a matter of *if* you want to learn; it is a matter of *when.* I promise you, it is much easier if *you* decide *when* and not let a crisis dictate the timing.

STEP 6:

Begin by formulating the questions. Confidently pursue the answers by asking as many questions as it takes. By asking questions you will begin to learn and take control of your destiny instead of being forced to learn as destiny controls you.

~7~

TAKING CONTROL

To grow, move forward and realize your dreams, you must take action and commit to the belief that you can do it.

"Desire is the key to motivation, but it's the determination and commitment to an unrelenting pursuit of your goal -- a commitment to excellence -- that will enable you to attain the success you seek."
Mario Andretti

You will succeed if you visualize the life you want and take the proper actions to bring you there. You will fail if you know what you want, but fail to take the actions necessary to get it.

Every woman has the ability to be financially independent. You simply need to set your goals, internalize them and take action to bring them to fruition. This is called *planning.* If you plan and take action, you will create a life you never dreamed was possible. Start by answering the following questions:

1. What does your current financial situation look like?

____

____

____

2. How does it make you feel?

____

____

____

3. If you continue on the same track, what will your financial situation look like 10 years from now?

____

____

____

4. What would you *like* your financial situation to look like currently?

____

____

____

5. How would this make you feel?

____

____

____

6. If you continued on this *preferred* track, what would your financial situation look like 10 years from now?

____

____

____

This should give you an idea of what you want out of life. Now you need to formulate a plan of action to achieve this vision. One thing you need to remember, however, is that all of the planning and action in the world will not be enough. You must have a positive attitude toward money. This is actually what we have been discussing throughout this section of the book: you and your attitude toward money. You must be comfortable with money and what it brings. You must believe you are worth the positive benefits of having financial independence and control, and that you have the potential of achieving it.

Think about a new mother looking into the eyes of her newborn. She sees a life full of potential. She sees the kind of life that she believes this child will have -- a life full of happiness, dreams, and financial security. We must remember these feelings, and then project that same image for ourselves. We must expect the best from ourselves.

You must plan your path. Remember, no one achieves financial success and control overnight. Financial success is planned and thought out carefully. Then action and determination pull the plan together.

These are the first keys to financial success. The result of this is control -- control over your life's direction, which I believe is what each of us wants. No one wants to be the victim of circumstance. Each of us wants to be the captain of her own ship.

STEP 7

Take action and begin planning, which will result in control. You are now able to break free of the past and your comfort zone. You can see the life you want, and you know that it is within your reach. It is ultimately control which determines the quality of life that you make for yourself.

SUMMARY AND CONCLUSION

"The future is not in the hands of fate,
but in ours."
Jules Jusserand

You have made it through Part I - Congratulations! If you followed the steps suggested, you are now 50% closer to achieving financial independence and becoming *a woman of wealth* than you were earlier.

You may wonder why we had to address the issues we did in Part I. I believe it is necessary for each of us to recognize our subconscious feelings and beliefs toward money matters. When we recognize these, we can deal with them consciously, put them into perspective, make rational decisions and take actions that lead us to independence and wealth.

You now know where you have been. Hopefully this has allowed you to gain some insight into where you are now. Take this knowledge and financial wisdom and carry it into the future. This knowledge will assist you throughout your life in making good financial decisions for yourself. It will also help you to assist the next generation of women.

You now need to go forward confidently, for your financial future is no longer in the hands of others or of fate, but in your own hands. Take the next step and reap the rewards.

Women's Financial Wisdom

How to Become a Woman of Wealth

PART II

INTRODUCTION

"There are risks and costs to a program of action - but they are far less than the long range risks and costs of comfortable inaction."
John F. Kennedy

The average woman spends more time planning dinner than she spends planning her future. In fact, only 2% of women have set goals for their lives and have established a plan of action to achieve those goals.

Napoleon Hill, one of the best financial, inspirational writers of all time, stated in his book, *Napoleon Hill's - A Year of Growing Rich,* "Unless you know what you want from life and are determined to get it, you will be forced to accept the mere crumbs left by others who knew where they were going and had a plan for getting there." *

All financially successful people have goals and a plan of action to help achieve those goals. Without them, they wouldn't be financially successful. Do

---

*Napoleon Hill, *Napoleon Hill's A Year of Growing Rich*, (New York: Penguin Group, 1993)

you think Bill Gates, one of the wealthiest men in the country, is without goals and a plan?

I am certain that he would not accept the crumbs from others. Are you willing to accept crumbs?

It is time to decide what you want from life and formulate *your* plan of action. To help you begin, answer the following questions:

1. **To accomplish your ideal financial situation, what individual goals would you set for the following?**

   a) Your income goal? ________
   b) Your savings goal? ________
   (ie: 10% of gross wages.)
   c) Your spending goal? ________
   (ie: 80% of net wages.)
   d) Your retirement goal? ________
   (ie: 80% of gross wages.)
   e) Other goals? ________

2. What benefits will you receive by accomplishing these goals?

____

____

____

____

3. What emotional changes will be necessary to accomplish these goals?

____

____

____

4. What physical resources will be necessary to accomplish these goals?

____

____

____

5. How much time will these goals take?

____

____

____

6. What steps do you need to take *daily* to accomplish these goals?

____

____

____

By answering the above questions, you have just created the foundation for your plan. Now all you need to do is add specific financial actions, which I will give you over the next few chapters. The result of these questions and the actions I give you will be a list of daily *to do's* for achieving your dreams.

Take a moment to write one of your main goals in red ink and big letters on a 3x5 index card. Repeat this for each goal you have. Under each goal, list the actions you need to take to achieve it. Some of these actions you have already identified. Write them down. As I provide other actions for you in the next few chapters, write them down as you come across them. When you are finished with this book, you should have a formulated plan of action.

Tape a copy of this plan of action to your bathroom mirror, your refrigerator, and any other spot where you would be likely to see it throughout the day. This will remind you constantly of the actions you need to be taking.

Eventually, these actions will become second nature to you and become habits. As they do, you will see your goals take shape and begin to be realized. You will see yourself becoming *a woman of wealth.*

~1~

THE RULE OF TEN

A portion of all you earn is always yours to keep.

"The best way to predict
the future is to invent it."
Alan Kay

Most rules in life are established to protect us. We all know *to look both ways before crossing the street,* and *never talk to strangers.* There are also financial rules that have been established for our protection. One such rule is the *Rule of 10.*

The *Rule of 10* simply states: ***save 10% of all you make.*** If you make $10, save $1. If you make $100, save $10. Many of us may already know this Rule as, *pay yourself first.* It really is good advice; and if you want to become a *woman of wealth,* you must practice this at all times.

When you take 10% off the top from all income you earn, you will be amazed with the results. When you place these funds in a *separate* savings account so that you don't use it by mistake, you will find this account growing at a more rapid rate than you could ever have hoped.

I have counseled many women who state vehemently that they *cannot* possibly take 10% off the top or there will not be enough funds to pay the bills. I always ask them to try it for a month. At the end of the month nine out of ten of these women have found that they didn't even notice the difference!

The reason for this is that we often match our spending to what is in our pocket. If we have an extra $10 in our pocket, we will always find a way to spend it. If we take the $10 out of our pocket, we won't spend it. We are simply removing 10% from our pocket *as if we never had it,* and soon we will find that we don't *need* it.

To explain this further, I will tell you about Sally. Sally was meeting her expenses without any trouble. She had a nice home, a new car, and just about everything she wanted. Sally, however, never saved a penny. She always told me there was no extra money to set aside in savings, and as soon as she earned more, she would be able to establish a savings plan for her retirement. Sally soon received a $2,000 a year raise, plus bonus. Sally, however, still did not save anything. Instead, her expenses simply increased to meet her new income. Her philosophy was, *"I'll save whatever is left at the end of the month."* There never was, however, anything left at the end of the month. Had she set aside funds at the beginning of the month, she would not now be scrambling to save as she approaches retirement.

If you wait to see what is left over, you will never save. It is crucial that you take this money right off the top and pay yourself first. You are worth it! *You* are your most important payment.

Another statement I often hear from women regarding their savings is that *a penny here and a penny there really isn't going to make a difference.* I believe differently.

If you save 10% from your paycheck weekly and you make $100 per week, you will save $10 each week. $10 saved every week for 10 years, placed in an account averaging 6% interest equals $7,120. Will this make a difference?

How about $20 per month? Save $20 per month during your working career of 40 years, and you will end up with $39,830 at retirement. Every bit helps.

I save my 10%, and I am teaching my children to save 10% of all they earn. They save 10% of their birthday money or any funds they receive. They are learning this valuable habit at an early age so that they will find it easier later in life.

$95.40 saved each month (just like a car payment or house payment), beginning at age 20, and placed in an account averaging a 10% return, will net $1,000,000 at the age of 65.

Try to remember this: even if you are past the age of 20 and might not be able to save $1,000,000 for yourself, it isn't too late for your children or grandchildren. Teach them well.

STEP 1:

Save 10% of all you earn. Place these funds in a separate account, and forget that they are there. This isn't *spending* money. It is *savings*. To save means to preserve and protect. Rules are also designed to protect. Therefore, this rule of saving is actually an act of protecting you. Make it a habit, and protect yourself.

~2~

DESIRE OR NECESSITY

Make sure you pay for your needs before you begin buying your wants.

"Reading about this and not practicing it, is no more effective than filling a prescription and not taking the pills."
Dr. Carl Simonton

In the last chapter I suggested that our expenses will always grow to equal our income. This is mainly due to two factors: First, if it is in our pocket, we spend it. Second, our perception of necessity is confused with desire.

We live in a society of immediate gratification, and many of us fall prey to its deceptive control over our lives. It confuses us to believe that all of our desires and wants are needs, and that our needs are indispensable.

A person could fill page after page with all her financial desires. She might want anything from a new automobile, to a new house, to an annual vacation in the Caribbean. Once these items have been obtained, a new list appears and replaces the old. Desires and wants are *infinite!* Needs, however, are *finite*. The trick is to determine which is which.

Let's begin with a list of *needs* or *necessities:*

<u>Expenses as a Result of Needs or Necessities:</u>

Savings (10%)	________
Automobile Payments	________
Child Care	________
Clothing	________
Education	________
Electricity	________
Gas	________
Groceries	________
Heat	________
Housing (Mortgage or Rent)	________
Insurance:	
Auto	________
Life	________
Home	________
Medical	________
Medical Expenses	________
Phone	________
Taxes:	
Federal	________
Property	________
State	________
____________	________
____________	________
____________	________
Total:	=======

The above is a list of basic necessities. You can add to this any item you feel is a real necessity for your particular circumstance. The list below is a list of wants or desires.

Expenses as a Result of Wants or Desires:

Cable TV	________
Dining Out	________
Entertainment	________
Gifts	________
Home Furnishings	________
Movies	________
Subscriptions	________
Vacation	________
____________	________
____________	________
____________	________
Total:	=======

This second list could literally go on forever with *new this and new that.* I obviously cannot list every conceivable desire; however, I have listed a few which most people place in their necessity column. These items are not necessities. Sometimes we may feel that cable TV is a real need, but it may not be.

Make your own list. Begin with those items that are *needs,* then begin to add those *desires* that are possible to obtain within your income range. Cross out the rest, or add them to your goals or wish lists for another day. Every time you go to purchase an item, stop and ask yourself, is this a *need* or *a desire*? If it is a desire, is it #1 on your desire list?

Most people refer to what we have just done as budgeting. In simpler terms, you are not allowing your desires to overextend you financially by turning them into needs.

STEP 2:

Continually save 10%, and use the remainder first for your needs. Once your needs are satisfied, determine which desires have the most importance for you. You must differentiate between desire and necessity every time you make a purchase, and be willing to forgo the immediate gratification of desire in order to build your wealth.

-3-

YOUR EARNING POWER

You can increase your ability to earn by increasing what you learn.

"You are successful the moment you start moving toward a worthwhile goal."
Chuck Carlson

How do you earn more when someone else controls your pay scale? How do you get that raise you need? How do you increase your earnings potential? It is very simple: *the more you learn, the more you earn.*

There are thousands of books on this topic alone. I have read several of them, and they all had a similar message -- if you learn all you can about your company and industry, soon you will be more valuable to your employer, which will result in more income. Without going into a lengthy lecture on how to increase your worth to your employer, I will illustrate this point by telling you a story about myself.

When I began working back in the 70s, I began as a secretary. I made approximately $12,000 a year. I thought it was great, but felt I was worth more. I knew how hard I worked. I knew I was doing a good job. My employer, however, felt this was fair pay for this position. In order for me to earn more I had to make myself more valuable to my employer. To do this, I had to learn more.

I began by learning the next position up from mine: the insurance position. I made sure that I was always available as a backup and took on work whenever possible. I then proceeded to obtain my State insurance license. Due to this initiative, I soon moved into the insurance position (with a raise). I took a similar approach with the brokerage position. I learned the job and then obtained the proper licensing. Again, I moved into this position (with a raise).

At this point I had learned all of the back-office operations in both the insurance and brokerage divisions. I was licensed and began working as an associate to our financial advisors. Even though I had the same licensing and was head of our trading operation, I was still viewed as a secretary by many of the advisors. Once again I had to look for ways to build my credibility and value to my company. As a result, I obtained more licenses, and began reading on every related topic I could find. I increased my knowledge and credibility in no time. My value to my employer was increased, along with my wages.

The problem began in the 80's when I married my husband. We decided that I would take a small base pay for my work, and he would support us financially. I decided to take no more than $20,000 per year as my wages. The money wasn't an issue for me; however, my inner sense of worth was *screaming* at me, telling me that I was worth so much more.

By now I was helping to run the entire company. I knew every position and was responsible for the company's financial situation. I was a vice president and on the Board of Directors of a public company, making $20,000 a year! So I made a deal with my husband and took myself off the payroll! I told him that I would take only a percentage of the income I generated for the company and would no longer take a salary. The first year I did this, I generated in excess of $200,000. I finally felt I was being paid what I was worth.

While not everyone is in a position which would allow a change like this, there are some things that anyone can do. Below are but a few. I guarantee, however, if you practice these, you will become more valuable to your employer and your wages will increase. If your employer does not offer the added wages, make sure to ask for them. Your employer will recognize how valuable you have become and will not want to lose you and will compensate you accordingly. If he/she does not, you have simply made yourself more valuable to a potential employer.

Here is a list with which to begin:

- Take more interest in your work and in your company.
- Learn everything you can about your company.
- Make a decision to turn off the TV and read about your business.
- Read about your company, its competitors, its business and industry.
- Look for ways to save your company money, and bring your ideas to the attention of those who have the ability to implement your innovation.
- Become an expert in an area where your company needs help. Learn all that you can, and obtain any licensing or exams necessary to assist you.

- Become more visible. Make your ideas and accomplishments known to those who have the ability to reward these ideas financially.

- Dress the part. If you're doing the work of a manager, or aspire to be one, dress like one. Always dress for the job you want, not the job you have.

- Think of yourself as self-employed. If this were your company, decide what you would do in order to make your company a success, and then do it.

STEP 3:

Bury your pre-conceived notions that someone else controls your earnings. You control your ability to earn. By learning more, and becoming more valuable to your employer, you increase your *earning power*. Don't sabotage yourself. Go the extra mile and reap the financial rewards.

~4~

MULTIPLICATION

We learn our math tables in school. Why do we forget them when it comes to our savings?

"Planning is bringing the future into the present so you can do something about it now."
Alan Lakein

In order to become *a woman of wealth* it is critical that you discipline yourself to save 10% of all your earnings, and control your expenses. Next, comes the importance of multiplying your savings. Saving is one thing. Putting your money to work is another.

Most women have savings accounts where they keep their liquid assets. This money typically earns 2 or 3 percent interest. The goal, however, is to have your savings earn the most it can without risking its principal. You could use money market funds, CD's, US Treasury Bonds or other similar investments. It is not the savings vehicle which is most important, but rather it is the income you build as a result of the vehicle you choose. A woman's wealth is not simply in her savings. It is in the income her savings produces.

If you are to obtain true wealth, you cannot simply save your funds and not put them to work. Your money needs to be multiplying and growing.

You put your money to work *now*, so *you* will not have to work as hard later.

Earning interest is an example of your dollars working for you. Interest is free! You didn't have to put in 40 hours to obtain it. You simply had to invest your dollars in an interest-bearing account.

As your money works for you, it works even harder as time goes on. The more time you have, the more interest your money acquires, and then something wonderful happens: your interest begins earning interest. This is called compound interest.

Below are a few examples of how important interest is to your savings:

The value of interest.

You have made a commitment to save $10 each week during your working career of 45 years. Unfortunately, you never invest this $10 but simply keep it in a *piggy bank* at your home. When you are ready to retire you will have saved $23,400.

Your neighbor Pat also saved $10 per week, but she placed her money into an account earning 6% per year. When she decides to retire, her account is worth $120,090 simply due to a 6% annual return.

The value of earning more interest.

Joan has $10,000 in her savings account today. She is earning 2% on her money and doesn't plan to touch it for 10 years. At the end of the 10th year, her account will be worth $12,189. If she had invested her money in a 6% interest bearing account, her account would be worth $17,908 at the end of the 10th year.

Are you so rich that you are willing to forgo the extra $5,700? You must always remember to make your savings work for you.

The value of investing at the beginning of the year.

Maybe you don't have $10,000, and it seems that this amount of money is a lifetime away. The only savings you have is the 10% you are setting aside. You decide to set $1,200 away each year. At the *end* of each year you take $1,200 and place it in an account earning 6%. You do this for 25 years. At the end of the 25th year your account would be worth $65,837.

If, however, you take the same $1,200 and put it in your account at the *beginning* of each year instead of the end, your account would be worth $69,787 at the end of the 25th year. By allowing your money to work for you all year, you accumulate an extra $3,950.

Becoming a woman of wealth is simply knowing how to always make your money work for you. You must make your money your slave, and not become a slave to your money.

STEP 4:

You must never be content to receive little or no return on your money. You must seek higher returns so that your money has the opportunity to work for you. You don't need to invest with considerable extra risk to accomplish this. You must simply let your money work smarter, not harder.

~5

PROTECTING YOUR FAMILY

Your family is your responsibility. Protect them.

"You can either take action, or you can hang back and hope for a miracle. Miracles are great, but they are so unpredictable."

Peter Drucker

Before you can even consider building a financial portfolio, you must make sure your financial foundation is solid.

Building your financial foundation is similar to building a foundation for a house. You always build a house on a strong, well-constructed foundation. If the foundation is weak, there is the risk that your house could collapse. This holds true for a financial portfolio as well. You never build a financial portfolio on a weak or half-built foundation. The foundation must be strong and solid.

By building a strong financial foundation you are simply protecting your family. Your foundation should consist of the following items:

Automobile Insurance

- Health Insurance
- Home Insurance
- Disability Insurance
- Life Insurance
- Liability Insurance
- Emergency Fund

Okay, so now I have probably lost you altogether. Just the mention of insurance often turns people off, but I'm here to tell you how critical it actually is.

Following are some examples to help you see the importance of each item:

Kim has a portfolio of $1,000,000; however, her foundation is not complete. She has no disability coverage. When she falls while skiing and breaks her back, she finds herself out of work for the next 5 years and unable to ever hold down a full time job. Her portfolio is eaten up because of her inability to earn similar income to what she was earning prior to her injury.

Nancy also has a portfolio of $1,000,000. She has decided to cut costs and only has the basic liability coverage of $150,000 on her house. Nancy forgets to put salt on her steps after an ice storm and a neighbor slips on her front step and is injured. Nancy's neighbor sees Nancy as a *cash cow* and sues her for several million dollars. Nancy's liability coverage only goes to $150,000. She ends up losing much of her portfolio to settle with her neighbor. Nancy should have had an umbrella (liability) policy to cover her to a greater extent.

Myrna is a homemaker and the wife of a physician. She is a stay-at-home mom, living in a $250,000 home and has a $100,000 a year lifestyle. Her spouse has a life insurance policy with coverage of $250,000. When he dies unexpectedly in a car accident, Myrna is faced with a $200,000 mortgage, college education for her son, and a $100,000 a year lifestyle she can no longer afford. She receives the $250,000 death benefit from the life insurance and invests it in an account earning 10%. This gives her income of $25,000 per year, plus she receives social security for her son. She has to change her lifestyle dramatically. She must sell her home and go back to work simply to support herself. If her husband had a $1,000,000 life policy, she would not have had to deal with these issues at such a difficult time in her life. $1,000,000 invested at 10% would allow her enough income each year to provide a similar lifestyle, maintain her home and assist her son in his college education.

A $1,000,000 life insurance policy is more common than you would think these days. In order to earn $100,000 a year, you would need to invest $1,000,000 at 10%. You should keep in mind, however, that you cannot always earn 10% on your money. As rates fall, it may require additional coverage. If you or your spouse earn $50,000 a year, you should have a $500,000 life policy at minimum.

You are not being greedy. You are protecting yourself and your family. You don't want your children to have to struggle to attend college, and you don't want to have to use all of your savings to pay the expenses while you are disabled. If even one of these areas is not protected, you are risking collapse of your entire portfolio.

Make sure that all areas are covered. We often complain about how much we pay for insurance coverage that we might never need; however, I have never once heard someone complain when they receive payment from their insurance company to replace a home they have just lost to a fire, or to replace a car after an accident, or to replace their income while disabled, or to pay for health expenses while sick. Insurance coverage is there for you when you need it to protect you, and it is the base of your financial foundation.

The last item in your foundation should be an emergency fund equivalent to 3 to 6 months' worth of your monthly expenses. This will protect you from short term problems or income loss. Keep this money fairly liquid for emergencies.

The sign of a good financial advisor is one who is not afraid to recommend the insurance coverage listed above. She or he understands the importance of them. You, too, must understand that insurance was created to protect you and your family. Make sure you are covered.

STEP 5:

Remove your dislike for insurance and understand its importance for your protection in life. Even if you don't want to protect yourself, you have a responsibility to your family and children to protect them. You must move beyond your feelings, face reality, and protect those you love.

~6~

YOUR FINANCIAL PARTNER

Choosing a financial partner is as important as choosing a spouse.

"I've learned one important
thing about living.
I can do anything I think I can -
but I can't do anything alone.
Create your team!"
Dr. Robert Schuller

As Dr. Schuller states in the above quote, "Create your team!" It is important that you understand that we all need help. It is difficult for any of us to do everything alone. Financial planning and investing is one area in which I can assure you, you cannot succeed alone. You are going to need to find a good financial advisor to assist you.

Finding the right advisor is crucial. I like to call the person you choose your financial *partner*, not just your financial advisor. Your relationship should be similar to a marriage. You don't have to love this person, but you do have to trust, respect and value his or her opinions and knowledge.

To begin the search for your financial partner, ask your friends, family and co-workers whom they would recommend. This is a good start. If you get the same name two or three times, make an appointment with that person. If you don't get a specific name, ask for names of firms in your area. You can also call the Bureau of Insurance and Department of Securities in your State and ask for a list of financial advisors in your area.

Once you have done this, you could conceivably have a pretty long list of names or companies. Financial planning is a hot industry right now, and everyone seems to be calling himself a financial advisor. Today, insurance agents, stock brokers, bankers, accountants and thousands of others are calling themselves financial advisors.

The scary part is that in 1996 approximately 2 out of 3 people managing money had never participated in a *Bear Market*. (*To help you understand what Bear or Bull Stock Markets are, imagine this: The Bull is charging forward, it is aggressive and moving fast. This is when the market is going up. When you hear about a Bear Market, think about a bear, retreating into his cave to hibernate. This is when the market is retreating, or going down.*)

Be careful of one-man shops, part-time advisors, or people who are only licensed to sell for one company or one type of product. Always look for a well established company with a team of advisors.

Remember, one person cannot know it all in today's environment. This is especially true for part-time advisors. There is no way that they can keep up with the ever-changing financial markets.

Another reason for avoiding sole-proprietor financial advisors is lack of backup. What happens if your advisor has a heart attack? Who will take care of your account? Who will figure out his or her filing system to find your files? You want to make sure that the company with which you do business will be around when you need it.

Anyone can call himself or herself a financial advisor, even individuals who are licensed only to sell one type of product (i.e.: only insurance or only securities.) I can guarantee you, if you go to an advisor who can sell only one type of product, that will be the *only* type of product in your financial portfolio! Make sure you are dealing with someone who can look at your portfolio objectively and choose the types of products that meet your needs, not those which meet his or her licensing constraints.

If you eliminate these types of advisors from your list, it should be forming nicely. Now that you have a few names or firms, the interview process begins.

Make appointments with the advisors or companies left on your list. Let them know that you are interviewing for a financial advisor and ask them specific questions. Remember, I said one of the secrets of knowledge was asking the right questions and having the right answers. To help you choose a qualified advisor I have prepared a checklist of questions for you to ask each advisor with whom you are considering doing business. I have also written the answer which you should be seeking.

Questions to Ask Your Potential Financial Partner

1. Do you have your life insurance license? (Yes)

2. Do you have your securities license (Series 7) through the NASD? (Yes - the Series 7 securities license is the most comprehensive of the general securities, and your advisor should have it. Recently, however, the NASD has established a new program of licensing which would entail your advisor having both a Series 6 and Series 62. This is also an acceptable answer.)

3. Are you registered with the State as a Registered Investment Advisor? (Yes)

4. Are you or your firm registered with the Securities and Exchange Commission as a registered investment advisor? (Yes)

5. Are you a full-time advisor? (Yes)

6. Do you work with a company that has more than one financial advisor? (Yes)

7. Is your firm financially sound? (Ask for a balance sheet and make sure the company has more assets than you do!)

8. Does your firm have a disclosure statement which outlines the names and background of personnel, potential conflicts of interest and methods of compensation? (Yes. If the person is a registered advisor, this should be available to you. Ask for a copy and read this over after you have left.)

9. How long have you been in the business of advising clients? (I prefer someone with 10 years' minimum experience; however, less can be acceptable depending on his/her background, experience and team of specialists working with him/her.)

10. Do you represent more than one company? (Yes)

11. Are you either a Certified Financial Planner (CFP) or a Chartered Financial Consultant (ChFC)? (The answer here doesn't necessarily have to be yes. He or she should, however, be working toward this designation and be working with other CFPs and ChFCs within the company.)

12. Have you or your firm ever gone through personal bankruptcy? (No)

13. Have you or your firm ever been censored by the Securities and Exchange Commission (SEC) or the National Association of Securities Dealers (NASD)? (No)

14. Have you or your firm ever been reprimanded by the State Securities and Insurance Regulators? (No)

15. Have you ever been sued by a client? (No. If the answer is yes, find out the reason for the suit and what the outcome was.)

16. What is your CRD number and the company's CRD number with the NASD? (With these two numbers you can call the National Association of Securities Dealers at 1-800-289-9999 and find out if there is anything on their records that would stop you from doing business with this firm or individual.)

17. Why should I do business with you and your firm? (Make sure you are comfortable with the person and the answer you receive.)

18. Is there any other information that you could give me that would help me in making my decision? (He or she might provide you with marketing material or references. Anything extra will aid you in making a final decision. Please note, however, many financial advisors will not give you names of clients to call for references. Due to the confidentiality of this area, many individuals do not want their names disclosed.)

Thank the person for his or her time, and take the information and leave. Don't make a decision on the spot. Take your time to read through the information and reflect on how each potential advisor made you feel. Do, however, set a deadline for making a decision.

STEP 6

Evaluate all of the information you have just obtained. Narrow your choices down to those advisors that had most of the *right* answers and made you feel the most comfortable. Then you must follow your inner instinct. Are you comfortable with this person? Do you feel you could work well with this person? Do you dare to speak your concerns without a feeling of intimidation? If so, you are on the right track and you have just found a partner to help you become *a woman of wealth.*

SUMMARY AND CONCLUSION

"The achievement of your goal
is virtually assured the moment
you commit yourself to it."
Mack R. Douglas

Remember back to the first time you ever drove a car. You were probably scared to death. Your car was big and powerful, and driving it meant that you were going to have to show an immense amount of responsibility. Yet your excitement and the thought of independence gave you the encouragement and determination to go on. You no longer would have to rely on someone else to take you where you needed to go, and as a result, you mastered driving the car. You took control and overcame your fear.

You need to do the same thing while taking on the responsibility for your financial future. You need to let your excitement and hope of independence overcome your fears. You will no longer need a driver. You will be the driver and the one in control of your financial destiny. You will have the power.

You will become the master of your financial future and not let your finances master you.

By reading this book you have just made your first investment. This is an investment in yourself. You have proven that you believe enough in yourself to take time to gain a bit of knowledge. You may not realize this, but the greatest wealth you could ever have next to health is the wealth of knowledge! Money may be lost or stolen, but knowledge will be with you forever. Knowledge also increases your wisdom. Therefore, I stress the importance of understanding that without knowledge and wisdom, there can be no wealth.

The saying, *a fool and his money are soon parted,* is about a person who has no financial wisdom. Those who have no wisdom will never be able to control their financial destiny. Those who take the time to gain financial wisdom will have already made one of the greatest and most powerful investments they can. It will be an investment in themselves and their knowledge. These are the women who control their own destiny and become *women of wealth.*

I invite you to join the thousands of women who are *women of wealth.* These are women who want to control their own financial future and are taking steps to gain as much knowledge and wisdom as possible. You could be one of them.

Since you have made it this far, I'd like to ask that you take one more action and let me know how you are doing. Let me know where you have been and where you expect to go. I'd love to hear about your goals and your dreams. Your letters will be forwarded to me if you address them to:

Ivy Gilbert-Vigue
Women & Investing Inc.
222 Kennedy Memorial Drive
Waterville, ME 04901

Or, if I can help you with your financial goals and planning, write me at the address above, call me at (207) 873-0691, or e-mail me at *vigue@mint.net.*

You can also reach me by accessing The Women's Pages web site's financial section at *www.womens-pages.com.*

May financial wisdom be with you always, and may you soon become a *woman of wealth.*

"May the road rise to meet you,

may the wind be always at your back,

may the sun shine warm on your face,

the rain fall softly on your fields;

And until we meet again,

may God hold you in the palm of his hand."

Gaelic Blessing

To Our Readers:

Thank you for Purchasing *Women's Financial Wisdom - How to Become a Woman of Wealth.* We hope you enjoyed reading it. For your convenience we are enclosing this order form for additional copies of *Women's Financial Wisdom* for your friends and family.

Order Form

Name: ________________________________
Street: ________________________________
City, State, ZIP ___________________________

Please send to the above address:

____ copies of *Women's Financial Wisdom*
($12.95 each)

Please add $3.00 for shipping.

Enclosed is my total: $__________

Send check or money order to:
Ivy Gilbert-Vigue
Women & Investing Inc.
222 Kennedy Memorial Drive
Waterville, ME 04901